Imitation Crab

poems by

Katie Vagnino

Finishing Line Press
Georgetown, Kentucky

Imitation Crab

Publisher: Leah Huete de Maines

Editor: Christen Kincaid

Cover Art and Design: Jen Schultz

Author Photo: Lisa Venticinque

Order online: www.finishinglinepress.com
also available on amazon.com

Author inquiries and mail orders:
Finishing Line Press
P. O. Box 1626
Georgetown, Kentucky 40324
U. S. A.

Table of Contents

I have already lost touch with a couple of people I used to be.

—Joan Didion

And so I set about being myself, which required a great amount of observing the behaviors of Others, so that I could become the authentic decapod I desired to be...I would do my best, as the waters receded twice a day, to find a private tide pool in which to practice. Scuttle and pick, float and scuttle, pick and eat, scuttle and pick, eyestalks up high, eyestalks down low—oh, it was futile! I knew how stupid I looked, I, who had been born a decapod and would die a decapod but had no idea how to be a decapod without constantly thinking about how to be a decapod—so stupid, so stupid, so stupid! I was the fakest being with ten legs who ever scuttled the earth, and I would never be myself.

—Ben Hahn

ONE

Imitation Crab

With practice you can learn to spot a fake—
sloppy sleight of hand, or a smile too slick
gives it away. The truth is what we make

of the mess we inherit, lessons we take
away from blowing red-faced on trick
candles. With practice you can spot fake

tans and breasts, crocodile tears at a wake,
the forged signature on a permission slip
or counterfeit check. The truth makes

frauds of us once we see what's at stake:
pastel Monopoly money, stacked thick.
Children can always spot a fake,

detect the bullshit in stories half-baked.
They know the Santa at the mall is not authentic
(the phony beard gives him away) but they make

believe and sit on his lap because the truth shakes
them to the core: Everyone lies and nothing is magic.
With practice, you can tell the real from the fake
but unless you're the crab, what difference does it make?

Mise-en-scène

You pantomime making breakfast
while your husband does his best impression
of a man who likes his wife's coffee.

Is your line "Have a good day at work"
or "Don't forget the dry cleaning"?

You can't remember, so instead cross upstage,
and ask him to take the dog you don't have
for a long walk. He adlibs a kiss
on the cheek and asks about dinner
as he grabs a wax banana from the centerpiece.

Without conflict, there is no drama:
Either Aristotle or your therapist said that.

Whatever you do, don't mention the character
who never arrived, the room repainted red
from robin's egg blue, your sister's hand-me-downs
you gave to Goodwill.

Remember, it's like they say on airplanes:
The closest exit may be behind you.

Souvenir

At the museum gift shop
we searched for the perfect artifact—
something to remind us of the afternoon
spent lost in the galleries, marveling
at how well-preserved objects
in controlled environments can be.

Among the charmingly useless keepsakes
(Fabergé egg-shaped soaps, a book
on the history of buttonholing) you told me
"souvenir" comes from the French irregular verb:
to remember. "You speak French?" I said.
We left without buying anything and you left

a month later. Now I souvenir
your cleft chin and the skyline of books
stacked along your bedroom floor. I souvenir
how abruptly we became unnecessary
to each other, like the bronze paperweight
in the shape of Degas's ballerina
you told me not to waste my money on.

Your Dreams Explained

Rotting teeth mean money troubles,
molars loose in the mouth like coins
rattling in a car cup holder,
never enough for the toll.

If you dream of being a fish,
a trout, say, swimming upstream,
you might be anxious about work
or the fact that your wife's skin

suddenly reminds you of scales—
you catch yourself wondering
how she'd look hooked by the gums.

Waking up wet with visions
of Ted from next door means
you'd like to have sex
with Ted from next door.

Vegetables represent repressed anger
toward your mother, who is to blame
for your cauliflower complexion,
your distaste for cooked fruit.

Flying is a sign of a lover's betrayal.
You are gravity,
abandoned.

The Worst Metaphors for Our Relationship

Court transcript with the juicy parts redacted
Banquet hall buffet   wisdom teeth impacted

An ambulance driving with its siren off
Our once-firm mattress now going soft

Boring B-roll on the director's cut
Drug trial placebo   pay-per-view smut

Marathoner on mile twenty losing steam
Chernobyl, Pompeii, Hiroshima   a dream

Dissolved upon waking   a play with no plot
A gift basket of fruit just starting to rot

Passed out before twelve on New Year's, too drunk
To get it up   a flat tire, no spare in the trunk

A mine of conflict diamonds   soufflé that won't set
A sing-song sonnet of rhyming couplets

Dead Dog

Zach, the class tattle, saw it first:
mess of slick black fur and bones,
blood on the road.

"Dead dog!" he hollered. Horse flies
haloed his head and we all craned
our necks to get a look.

"Sit back down!" yelled the bus driver
but we ignored him. For once I was glad
the windows didn't open.

"Poor thing," my mother said that night,
brushing my hair before bed. I don't know
if she meant me or the dog.

Oxford, Mississippi

I remember crawling under fences, your skin browning
in the August heat and your honeysuckle sweat.
The sun smoldered down on us, cigar tip in the sky.

I remember walking by the stream, admiring its clutter
of dragonflies, cattails, tin cans. I wanted to sink
my head in the silt and swallow the filthy water.

I remember nights on my roof, first with you, then others
I kissed till my lips blistered, waiting for dawn
to ignite the horizon in shocks of pink and grey.

I remember you pacing on my porch that last morning.
You looked at me like you did when we climbed the dead willow—
You cried for my ruined white dress, the mud in my hair.

Still Life

We fall into each other like swirls of paint
colliding on paper. The canvas of your body
I color with my own, lips staining
your chin, cheek, torso. Brush strokes
from your lashes—I inhale sharply—
and our pillowcases shimmer like twin moons.

Summer collapses into autumn and the moon
lingers longer each night, painting
scenes of winter in our minds, sharpening
the need to stay close, keep heat in our bodies.
We sit on your porch, the breeze stroking
chimes above our heads. The future stains

my dreams while the past stains
yours; we reflect each other's pain like moons.
Still, every evening at the stroke
of six, we clink glasses, paint
our story together in bright colors. Like bodies
of water separated by miles of desert, sharp

thirst clenches our throats, sharper
than silence. Once I asked why tears "stain"
faces and pillows. Our bodies
were tangled in bed, a hangnail moon
glowing through the blinds. "Paint
leaves a mark, but tears?" Stroking

my hair, you said you didn't know (stroking
my hair was your way to soothe my sharp
tongue). The side of the house you painted
the year the cicadas came is now stained,
covered in craters like the moon.
I studied you that day, how your body

arched to meet the wood. Your body—
I think of it sometimes when I stroke

myself with the blinds open so the moon
can watch. The ache is sharp
each morning when I see the sky stained
with another day, rot infecting the paint

on the part of the house where your body cut a sharp
shadow. I still want to stroke your paint-
stained back, on your skin trace little moons.

How to Explain Death to Your Daughter

Tell her on a cloudless afternoon—
a Sunday in November, maybe,

after the leaves have fallen
and the ground's first hard freeze,

or during spring's first inkling
before the buds or birds are back.

When she asks questions
that are impossible to answer,

touch the top of her perfect head
and say that death is necessary, as natural

as sugar dissolving in a glass of lemonade
leaving its essence to linger.

May Day

In debutante gowns of ivory brocade and lace
we parade across the lawn and curtsy to the crowd in pairs,
daisies braided in our hair.

Our brothers and boyfriends watch from the sidelines,
snickering at the girls who stumble and those they say
shouldn't be wearing white.

A Copland song begins the dance. Around the maypole,
we weave and unweave the satin ribbons patiently
as an army of Penelopes.

One girl is crowned Queen and handed a bouquet
of baby's breath and roses while the rest of us
hide our heartbreak.

Our mothers clap the hardest. They know how it feels
to be on the cusp of eighteen when everything still
seems effortless as a daffodil.

The Storm

Caught in the maw of it,
it's easy to believe
in God's opposite:
absence of tenderness,
winter fury whistling
like a thousand tin cans
dragged from a fleet
of wedding hearses,
rice in the tire ruts.

On nights like this
when clouds upstage
the stars, I dream
I am lightning,
or a cigarette lit
too long, my body
a lighthouse, beacon
made of bone.

Portrait of the Common Loon by an Unknown Artist

In this depiction, she looks unoffended
by the designation of ordinary,
a label assigned to her by some scientist
who cannot fly or live among lily pads,
who must wear clothes to keep warm,
whose calls often go unanswered.

She gazes off left, her infrared eye
focusing on something in the middle distance
beyond the frame: her mate or a predator, perhaps,
or a motor boat sending ripples across the bay.
Still, she remains unruffled, content with herself
and at peace with her place in the water.

The artist who painted her can relate—
Why sign your work when it is unremarkable
except in its proficiency, its accuracy
in rendering an everyday bird
going about its business, unresentful of
rarer creatures more deserving of attention?

Vera vs. the Butterflies

The eastern side of every minute of mine is already colored by the light
of our impending meeting. All the rest is dark, boring, you-less.
        —letter from Vladimir Nabokov to his wife, Vera, 1937

She had already lost him
and now his winged darlings
were hers to keep or kill.

She shared his fascination
with fragility and flight,
but walking in the woods

alone, armed with the net
he had given her, noting
each abandoned chrysalis,

unusual flecks of blue
on a *Parnassius apollo,*
she knew they had to go.

A book suggested pinching
thorax between thumb
and middle finger to snap

the exoskeleton for a quick
death, but she couldn't bear
their blood on her hands.

Suffocation in a kill jar—
too inhumane. She decided
finally to freeze them, let the air

do her dirty work. Watching
their wings pulse to stillness,
she imagined his delight

at the sudden flutter
of company, diaphanous
prologue to their reunion.

TWO

Raw Bar

Among the lemon crescents and crushed ice,
A dozen Duxbury oysters, still alive—
I pry them from their shells, dollop twice
With cocktail sauce and swallow. After five
I'm almost full, salt stinging my lips, till
A sip of water brings my hunger back:
Armed with a tiny fork, I make the kill,
Spilling brine like blood. They taste metallic,
Like oceanic coins harvested in steel
Cages alongside their mussel and clam
Cousins. What, if anything, do they feel
When cracked open by a sous chef's hands,
Arranged by size on a plate left to right,
Sliding down my throat without a fight?

Small Mammals of Treehaven

What is life like for the least weasel?
Does he mean the most to anyone?

He should be scurrying
through Northwoods underbrush
sniffing out lesser rodents,
living his best wild weasel life.
Instead he's trapped here
beneath a sheet of plexiglass
like a sad, furry hotdog
incapable of menace.

To his right sits a star-nosed mole
with claws like acrylic press-on nails
that look too long to be natural.
His namesake snout protrudes
like a vacuum cleaner attachment.
Were he alive, he'd surely smell
the five varieties of shrew
(pygmy, masked, water,
arctic, northern short-tailed)
pinned alongside him, preserved
for children on field trips to marvel.

Ode to Virtues

Patience is the ponytailed girl you hated in high school
who always raised her hand right as the bell rang.

Prudence, that self-righteous nun, whacks the back
of your neck for dozing off during morning prayer.

Charity paces by the bus stop but never gets on
while you pretend to pat your pockets for change.

Hope is a pet store parrot squawking platitudes:
Hang in there! Have a nice day!

Faith is the neighbor who owes you money
though you can never remember exactly how much.

And whatever happened to Chastity? Last you heard,
she was still dancing at that strip club out by the airport.

Bullseye

You went to Coney Island to get a tattoo,
        stopped in at the freak show first.
Lobster Boy pretended to cry
        while the Rubber Lady rolled her eyes
and wrapped a fishnetted leg around her neck.

"Dear, we must watch and pray,"
        a bum on the boardwalk said.
He asked your name;
        you gave him a quarter, said you wished
the line for the Cyclone was shorter.

The psychic with psoriasis yawned, then rubbed
        her belly chakra. She lit up a cigarette,
said she hadn't had her dinner yet,
        but could guess your weight
if you sat on her lap.

Who has time for the Wonder Wheel
        you wondered as you walked by.
You couldn't help but stare
        at the rusty cages suspended in air.
At last it's time to get what you came for—

the needle's inked and aimed
        at your chest. Soon you will be marked
with concentric circles around your heart,
        so no one can mistake what you are:
a walking human target.

Year of the Rat

Happiness is right beside you
>   my fortune cookie claims
>   but you disappeared to piss
>   right before the bill arrived
>   so it must be hiding among
>   the orange slices or buried
>   in rice studded with shrimp
>   the size of pennies.

Learn Chinese
>   the little scroll commands,
>   followed by translations
>   for "hotel" and "chicken"
>   and a list of lucky numbers,
>   all of them prime.
>   I eat my cookie,
>   then crack open yours:

Land is always on the mind of the flying bird
>   Before I can decide who's the bird
>   in this metaphor, you emerge
>   from the men's room triumphant
>   like you accomplished something
>   and wink at the waitress
>   while helping yourself
>   to the free mints.

Good Friend

Empty carbs, she says with a nod to the roll on her bread plate. She asks what color my nails are. *The More the Berrier*, I say. *You know me, I always go for the pun polish.* We study the menu in silence. *Today's on me*, she says, *just because.* I order a double martini and the lobster special although we both know I'm allergic to shellfish. Her lipstick's new, and she says the shade's called Blood Orchid. *There's no such thing as a blood orchid*, I tell her. *Sure there is. What are you, the orchid expert? No*, I say, *but you know what I am an expert on? YOUR HUSBAND'S COCK.* Her face turns lobster red, and she does something that looks like spitting but sounds like laughing so I laugh and the busboy refilling our water glasses laughs with us, too. I ask him for another roll. When she goes to the ladies' room, I slip the waiter my credit card. *My treat*, I say with a conspiratorial wink. *What a good friend,* he says.

In My Twenties

I thought every song was about me
I loved with a toddler's ferocity
I had too many shoes and not enough socks
I fantasized about my funeral
I lamented not being a wunderkind
I wished everything could heal at the speed of skin
I took too many taxis
I avoided the dentist and doing laundry
I flirted with men I had no interest in
I didn't vote in primaries
I lost things all the time
I wanted to look my age
I thought about selling my eggs
I pretended not to believe in God
I didn't drink enough water
I kept a dream journal
I tried cocaine
I hated beer
I tipped generously
I slept too much
I exercised too little
I wanted to get into a bar fight, have my face slapped by a stranger
I think I could have used a good slap when
I was in my twenties

Cook Until Done

*For my parents, who met in an adult education class called
"Cooking for Singles"*

On the first day, they made consommé.
The way his hands cracked the eggs,
Whipped their whites into a frenzy
Stirred something inside her.

The way his hands cracked the eggs
Made her wonder how he'd handle her.
Something stirred inside her
When he finally asked her out on a date.

He wondered how she'd handle herself
When he ordered Chianti at dinner.
On the date, he asked all the usual things,
Noticed her eyes were hazel like his.

He ordered more Chianti at dinner when
She said their matching initials were a sign
And noticed his eyes were hazel like hers.
He stroked her hand, offered to drive her home.

She said their matching initials must be a sign,
Picturing pairs of monogrammed towels.
He stroked her hand, invited her to his home.
Eight months later she was still there

Picturing pairs of monogrammed towels.
Watching him was like waiting for water to boil.
Eight months later she was still there
Without a ring, not getting any younger,

But a watched pot never boils.
At last she proposed an ultimatum:
"I need a ring. I'm not getting any younger."
That September, he caved in

At last to her ultimatum: a proposal
To consummate their love in marriage.
Eighteen Septembers later, it all caved in;
Both were whipped, but the frenzy was gone.

Useful Animal

...myself as a self, you know, not merely as a woman, or that useful animal a wife and mother...
              –Charlotte Perkins Gilman

The night before the surgery
I threw my breasts a goodbye party.
They deserved a proper send-off,
commemoration for their years
of cumbersome service.

"But what about breastfeeding?"
my mother wanted to know.
The surgeon told me to prepare
to be possibly unable to provide
milk for children I might never have,
that I could be sacrificing
the sensation of being suckled
by my barely sentient baby.
And for what? To wear cuter bras
and sleep on my belly like a sloth,
that adorably useless animal?

My best friend bought a cake
with tits as big as mine
from an erotic bakery,
let me cut the first slice.
I like to think it was a man
who baked it—I imagine him
imagining me topless,
delicately crafting my areolas
in pink buttercream, his erection
trapped under the apron ironed
by his wife that morning.

Dear Meathead

It's hard to believe you
have chromosomes in common
with the men I typically date:
writers, musicians, artists and
other assorted types too gentle
to call me my proper names—
Princess, Tease, Sometimes-Bitch.

I wonder, what would your chin feel like
burrowed between my breasts, my body
pinned against the graffitied wall
of a bar bathroom stall
till the bouncer yells at us
to get a room, and kicks us out
like the trash we are?

I'm straining to read the words
tattooed across the back
of your thick neck
(Nickelback lyric? Bible verse?)
when my high school Latin suddenly becomes useful:
Cogitationis poenam nemo patitur   there is no judge for thoughts.

Slut Villanelle

Moving from one man's bed to another's,
she reapplies lipstick, lets herself out the back door.
She spreads her legs so someone will love her

and she can say *I told you so* to her mother
who doesn't return her calls anymore
after she slept with a friend's husband, then another's.

Like wasps at a picnic, men at the bar hover.
She's done the rum-coke-and-fuck routine before,
spreading her legs, hoping someone will love her.

Maybe he's here tonight for her to discover.
Swaying her hips to the beat on the dance floor,
she twirls from one man's arms to another's

until dizzy, she sits on a stool to recover.
The bartender offers her water; someone mutters *whore*.
She crosses her legs, pictures her ideal lover:

He won't judge her for sharing her body with others.
Her mother said *Always leave them wanting more*.
Moving from one man's bed to another's,
she spreads her legs. Someone will love her.

You Were in My Dream Last Night

At least I think it was you
Your face was transposed
Like an anthem in a minor key
Fingers where your tongue should be

There was a baby speaking Spanish
Or maybe Portuguese
And a fish in a frame on the wall
Began to breathe

His gills broke the glass
And you went to clean up the mess
With your mouth-hands
Which began to bleed

Just as normal fingers would
But the blood, your blood
Was the color and consistency
Of beaten eggs just like

The ones you're making now
For us, for breakfast—or is it brunch?
You were in my dream last night
At least I think it was you

Junk Mail Ghazal

Pack your bags. Your best ticket deal landed right on time.
Meet fun-loving singles and save for a limited time

up to 76% on ink cartridges. Is 2021 your year to shine?
Be the ladies' talk of the town. Love is for a limited time.

Overpaying on your mortgage? Don't wait in line,
act now and you could make $24,000 in 24 hours' time.

Start learning to invest like a pro. No hidden fees or fines;
your money, when you want it, for a limited time.

You have been sent an e-kiss! Eliminate embarrassing tan lines
with this miracle spray. Enjoy free shipping for a limited time

on select orders, now thru Memorial Day. Get supersized
in the pants. Suffering from arthritis? For a limited time,

Cialis, Viagra, Adderall, Vicodin, Valium. Stop crime
with a hidden spy camera, no payments due at this time.

Does Sprint PCS offer you a clarity you can see? Find
out how to get the best rates on used cars—for a limited time,

no money down, 0% APR, cash back bonus, lifetime
warranty. Katie, these offers can be yours for a limited time.

Knife Work

Clutch me

        tight like a   kitchen knife

        when something   startles you from   sleep.

Hold me

        by the hilt   let me slit

        you open,   slide myself   inside.

When cutting,

        dull is   dangerous—

        a rusty blade   like curiosity   clotted.

Run your finger

        along my edge   to see

        how safe   my serration   is.

Sestina Noir

I didn't kill my husband whispers the blonde,
fingers drumming on the desk, her perfume
memorable, yet predictably floral. Her pencil-
thin lips curled into a smile. She had a figure
that begged—no, dared you to stare. *Justice?*
Is that what you're after? I ask, contract

in hand. She laughs. *I don't sign contracts.*
But I'm good for the dough. A bottle blonde,
no doubt, and there's no justice
for suckers like me. That damn perfume
was making me dizzy. She jots down a figure
with enough zeroes to break the pencil

so I can't say no. "Really? A pencil?
Wouldn't a private eye use a pen? Contracts
are only valid in ink, dear," says the figure
reading over my shoulder. "Another blonde?"
My wife sighs. Her scented lotion (never perfume)
makes me feel sexless, completely justified

in my fantasy. Readers don't care about justice
for mousy secretaries and losers who pencil
in face-time with a sleuth. They want perfume
mixed with sweat and bourbon, contracts
signed in blood by leggy blond
femme fatales like mine. My agent figures

I can turn legit soon, land a five-figure
advance for my first real novel—justice
for all my airport fiction. But back to my blonde:
He pulls her onto the desk; papers and pencils
scatter across the floor. The contract
blows out the window. Her perfume

will be on his clothes, and his fuming
wife won't say a word, figures

she can sue for breach of the marriage contract,
take the bastard for all he's worth. Justice
for cuckolded women everywhere. My pencil
breaks; reality, I realize, is marrying your blond

cousin's college roommate. Her bathrobe doesn't do her figure justice
and she hasn't been blond since she was born, but even without perfume
her contracted beauty is as gratifying as a just-sharpened pencil.

Homily

The day I lost my faith, some hungry other
took my place, whispered worship to a man

behind a grate collecting sins like stamps.
He coughs himself awake. Hail Marys

waft upward as spiders in the eaves
spin their webs in penitence. The hymns

without refrains are the hardest to remember
so I summon the familiar: the Fourth of July

family picnic, my older brother's freckled skin,
our father telling him to wear a hat, have some sense

for Christ's sake. God? He's in the unwashed
strawberries, the last sacrament of summer.

THREE

Fire Island Rubato

Out here the houses all have names:
Dune Well, Sea's the Day, Comfortably Numb.

From our porch we watch the divers
waiting for the slack tide.
There's safety in stillness
but they have to time it right, the pause
between the ocean's allegro and andante
when the waves hold their applause.

I feel like I have blood to spare today
so I show mercy to the mosquitoes,
let them draw me out in drops.
You slice a tomato with the precision
one might string a violin. You never
measure sugar or salt.

Long days decrescendo to nights.
The fireflies look fat enough to power
more than just themselves.

Sisters

July in Charleston: my sister cruises
with a low left tire, no spare, swats
my hand if I try to change the station.

We lurch into a 24-hour service station
and the pump boy's eyes cruise
over her suntanned skin, the sweat

collecting on her collarbone. I swat
flies, arch my back against our station
wagon, beg her to buy me a Grape Crush.

As we cruise out of the station, I lick sweat off the cold can.

Women at Forty

After Donald Justice

Women at forty
learn to slam loudly
doors opened by men
expecting something in return.

In elevators they unlearn
how to make themselves small
as they ascend past floors where
their grandmothers clerked or cleaned.

They have no use for mirrors.
They know their faces well from years
of applying lipstick in taxis,
public bathrooms, dark corners

of bars their mothers warned them about
when a bad reputation was the worst thing
they could imagine. Their daughters
will know better. When metaphors

fail them, as metaphors often do,
they will finally arrive at a place
where the only voice they listen to
is their own.

Jax Beach

My mother and I sip red wine from metal travel mugs. The sand beneath our feet is packed tight as brown sugar stored in the freezer, a trick she taught me to keep it from hardening.

"Henry the Eighth only beheaded two of his wives, you know," she says.
Actually, I did know that, I tell her.
"You always loved history," she says. I don't correct her.

My mother is a storm system, always moving, trying to claim some territory while the world shifts around her. Her father told Pollack jokes, but she knows better, or at least pretends to in decent company.

She asks me again if I remembered to put sunscreen behind my knees. I nod.

"Having children will change you," she says in a way that sounds both wistful and like a warning.

Nothing to Declare

My last morning in Porto de Pedras
I met a woman named Camilla on the beach.
In perfect English she apologized
for her terrible English. She taught me
the Portuguese word for hummingbird:
beija-flor, flower kisser.

I wish I'd asked her the name of the fruit
I tried at breakfast; it looked like a blueberry
but tasted tart like an unripe grape.
Later that day, on the bus to Recife,
I watched a little boy suckle a coconut
like it was his mother's breast.

Standing in the customs line, I tell myself
it's silly to feel homesick for a place
I barely got to know when something
warm and wet drizzles from my ear
down my neck like a well-kept secret
suddenly told.

The Salesmen

On the lot, the trade-ins bake
in the sun: Fords, Buicks, Chryslers,
chrome-plated steel behemoths,
some not much more
than a key and a heater.

But the salesmen know that any beater
is just a fresh coat of paint away
from being some sixteen-year-old's first
heartbreak when he guns through
a red light on his way to school.

Marty's on top this month. He smooth-talks
reluctant wives into taking test drives,
shows them pictures of his nephews,
pretends they're his kids. He's with one now
but stops mid-sentence and wanders

toward the exit because it's 4:00 p.m.
and he hears the jingle signaling the arrival
of Mister Softee. Commissions forgotten,
the salesmen line up like schoolboys by the truck,
dig through their suit pockets for change.

Every day they look forward to it,
the surge of that first cold mouthful
like putting foot to pedal,
how good it tastes to get
exactly what you paid for.

Pinball

Wrists tense, he propels the magnetic ball
      left   left   right
    left
                        away from the machine's underbelly.
It only takes a moment of distraction
        a glass breaks, or the jukebox skips
               and the game's over.

Bonus round: a silver second chance.
He pulls the plunger back,
      releases years of pent-up wants
        (his own place, a girlfriend, some goddamn respect)
    yes   yes   no
      no

        yes, everything is spring-loaded.

He plays like a man
who has seen his words   ricochet
    uselessly, like he learned   long ago
           the slam-tilt of experience

     has nothing to do

     with the score.

Elegy for Amy Winehouse

"Death by misadventure" was the cause
listed on the coroner's report,
one last blackout that couldn't be fixed
by flipping a fuse switch.

No Tabasco and tea, hair of the dog,
or stomach pumping. This time
the battle between blood and booze
went the other way and she never woke up.

The tabloids that hounded her
all her short life said she was found
by her bodyguard. Apparently, he mistook
her not breathing for a nap.

Amy, your voice is like honey on my nerves tonight.
I bet you looked good even at the end—
cat-eyed and beehived, the dissonant note
in the chord that never resolves.

Chrysalis

For the Grayson women

In Aunt Susie's kitchen, three women flutter
like agitated moths, discussing movies and weather
but never men or politics. Susie, armed with a bottle
of Tabasco and wearing a shirt that says "Gravity's
a Bitch," checks on the brisket. Her red
nails match mine and my mom wonders

if we planned it that way. Hungry, I wonder
if we'll eat before ten, if the flakes fluttering
down will stick. On the radio, Red
Allen croons about Stormy Weather.
Nana, ninety and reliable as gravity,
rises from her nap. "Are two bottles

going to be enough?" my mom asks, a bottle
of Zinfandel in her hands. Nana wonders
aloud if the store's still open; the gravity
of the situation sets in. Amid the flutter
of concerns about the inclement weather,
I pour myself a generous glass. The red

wine warms my throat, soothing as Red's
voice. Mom signals to me: Pass the bottle.
Two hours later, as they argue over whether
I should keep trying to be an actress, I wonder
if I'll ever learn to cook brisket, if the flutter
I feel is from the wine or the pull of gravity

in my chest. A curious thing, gravity,
I think as I watch my mom and her sister wipe red
stains from their lips. The snow is no flutter,
it's a full-blown storm. Nothing stays bottled
up forever. "Sometimes I wonder..."
Nana trails off. I want to ask her whether

she believes in second chances, whether
she fears death, what's beyond the grave.
But I say nothing. Susie laughs, "I wonder
if we have room for dessert—I've got red
velvet cake." The brisket and both bottles
of wine are gone. In a minute, I will flutter

off with the empty bottles. I'll overhear them lamenting gravity's
effect on their weathered bodies and comparing books recently read
while I flutter around the kitchen like a firefly, lit within from wonder.

Algorithms

I.

Only after discovering a common denominator
can two come together cleanly

Remainder implies something left over
or left out
conspicuous

Like how I felt on the last day of fourth grade
when I found out the answers had been in the back
of my math textbook all along

II.

The best kind of problem to be is an unsolvable one
and if you end up becoming a fraction
you should strive to be improper

III.

I can't remember how to find the slope of a line
but I know it has to do with distance
how far from one point to the next
how steep the journey

IV.

O to be a perfect integer
smug in the knowledge of my wholeness

Wunderkind

At his first lesson, the teacher nearly wept,
clutched the child as if he were a winning
lottery ticket. From that day on, he kept
playing; everyone said it was the beginning
of a great career. After concerts, he would rise
to greet the hordes of people waiting in line
to touch his hands, marvel at their tiny size.
His parents said they knew it was a sign
when they played piano concertos, he would kick
inside. Flashbulbs popped; the boy smiled,
posed for photos, even when he was sick
of hearing strangers say they had driven for miles.
On their programs, he always wrote the same:
God bless you for listening and then his name.

When adolescence came, he practiced less,
found other uses for his nimble fingers.
Arpeggios became labored; bass clefs
mocked him with their smirks. He lingered
after school to avoid going home where
his mother waited, sheet music in her hands.
Exasperated, one day she spat *How dare
you waste your gift.* She could not understand
his need to be normal, just someone's prom date,
someone's friend. After college, he took a job
behind a desk, moved to a town in another state.
Does he ever miss the adoring mob?
Only when colleagues stop by his cube to ask
Wow, where did you learn to type like that?

Simple Procedure

Is someone coming to get you they ask
  as I fill out my medical history,
decline the optional counseling.
They take some blood to be sure.

I fill out my medical history
and opt for local anesthesia
after they take some blood to be sure.
They tell me it's a simple procedure.

I opt for local anesthesia;
I don't want to be unconscious.
They tell me it's a simple procedure
so there shouldn't be any complications.

I don't want to be unconscious.
The nurse gives me a bin for my clothes,
says there shouldn't be any complications.
I change into a backless gown,

give the nurse my bin of clothes.
In a windowless room
I wait in my backless gown,
read the handwritten notes on the bulletin board.

In a windowless room
the nurse encourages me to write something,
or read the handwritten notes on the bulletin board,
most of which are apologies to Jesus.

The nurse encourages me to write something,
says it might make me feel better.
I don't think Jesus wants or needs my apology.
I change my mind, ask to be knocked out;

It might make me feel better.
The nurse makes a note on her clipboard

that I changed my mind, asked to be knocked out.
Next I remember waking up, groggy and bleeding

as the nurse makes a note on her clipboard.
There's a pad between my legs and
I remember waking up groggy the first time I bled,
bewildered by what my body could do.

There's a pad between my legs and
the nurse gives me a lollipop, walks me down the hall.
My body is bewildered but
the nurse says my blood sugar's just low.

She gives me another lollipop. Down the hall
a girl paces back and forth, rubs her eyes raw.
Her blood sugar must be low, too.
Is someone coming to get you I ask.

Homewrecker

You can't blame the hornets for being perturbed.
For months, maybe years, their nest had hung there,
tucked behind the screen door's hinge, undisturbed

until you discovered it. I whispered a prayer
while you, armed with a rolled-up magazine,
demolished what had been made with care.

I would have stung you. Maybe it was mean
of me to laugh, but the way your nostrils flared
as you swung your arms, and your posture—

threatening, yes, but more clumsy than fierce—
reminded me of myself at fifteen, unsure
of my breasts, my voice, my nose piercing.

Their home destroyed, you smiled, satisfied.
The threat was gone, or at least exiled outside.

Nocturnal

Night descends and the city starts to sweat.
You call me the wrong name, but I don't care.
I think I love you though we've only just met.

Police sirens wail an angry duet,
a Doppler opera swirling through the air
as night descends and the city starts to sweat.

You offer to light my cigarette
and we grope like teenagers, desire laid bare.
I think I love you though we've only just met.

A homeless man mumbles a threat
to the deserted alley as the unfair
night descends. The city starts to sweat

drops of *yes* and *now*. My lips are wet;
yours are somewhere in my hair.
I think I love you and we've only just met

but this might be as close as I'll ever get
so I'll take my rapture with a little despair.
Night descends and the city starts to sweat;
I think I love you—don't leave me yet.

Learning Curve

I don't remember learning how to wrap
a gift, who taught me how to tie the string
around my fingers, with a scissors curl
the ends. Tying shoes I'll credit to Dad,
along with telling time and jokes, balancing
a checkbook, chopping onions without crying.

In fifth grade, Val showed me how to run
a razor across my legs, warned *Watch out
around the ankles.* French kissing: the honor
goes to a wiry boy whose name was James
(or John?) who slid his timid tongue along
my gums, placed his hand on my hairless knee.

You can break a promise and be forgiven
I picked up from my mother, as well as how
to flirt while knotting a necktie around
your lover's throat. Lying I figured out
on my own. Little lies first, like *I haven't
felt this way before*, then bigger, hungrier
untruths: This glass will be my last; I never
wanted children; I am not a poet.

Acknowledgments & Thanks

Earlier versions of some of the work in this collection previously appeared in the following publications: *Poetry City, USA*: "Souvenir"; *Unsplendid*: "The Worst Metaphors for Our Relationship"; *Measure*: "Vera vs. the Butterflies"; *The Raintown Review*: "Wunderkind"; *Poetry Quarterly*: "Your Dreams Explained"; *Waterways*: "Cook Until Done," "Chrysalis," and "Learning Curve"; *Volume One*: "Imitation Crab," "Mise-en-scène," and "Still Life"; *nibble*: "Sisters"; *nthWORD*: "Ode to Virtues"; *The Furnace Review*: "Oxford, Mississippi"; *Words Apart*: "Raw Bar" and "The Storm."

"How to Explain Death to Your Daughter" was featured on Twin Cities Metro Transit as part of the 2017 Impressions contest and later published in the *Saint Paul Almanac*. "Fire Island Rubato" was one of 12 poems chosen for the 2015 Eat Local, Read Local program sponsored by UW-Milwaukee's English Department.

I'd like to thank the following people for their contributions to this book: Jen Schultz, Lisa Venticinque, Jon Loomis, Emily Anderson, Sonia Greenfield, Ben Hahn, and everyone at Finishing Line Press.

I am indebted to my family—Vagninos, Graysons, McGinnises, Yardleys, Pages, Richters, and Tituses—for their endless love and support. Special thanks to my teachers and mentors, especially John Skoyles, Christine Casson, Dan Tobin, Gail Mazur, Bruce Taylor, Charles Martin, and J.D. McClatchy. I'm also grateful for the encouragement and friendship of BJ Hollars, Joel Pace, Molly Patterson, Alice Swenson, Katie Poquette, Karla Lien, Jon Lehman, Zach Huelsing, Sarah Funke Butler, Emilia Seay Allen, David Bayliss, Alysoun Kegel, and Jill Snyder.

Finally, thank you, Jake, for being my person. You tell me often that I am a star and I can say with absolute certainty that I shine brighter because of you. I love you.

Katie Vagnino is a poet, educator, and writer originally from St. Louis, Missouri. She graduated from Yale, where she studied with poet and Yale Review editor J.D. McClatchy, and earned her M.F.A. in Creative Writing at Emerson College.

Katie's poetry has appeared in more than a dozen literary journals including *Measure, Unsplendid, The Raintown Review*, and *Poetry City, USA*. In 2017, her poem "How to Explain Death to Your Daughter" was featured on Metro Transit buses and trains in the Twin Cities. As a freelancer, her work has been published in the *Minneapolis Star Tribune, The Verge, Time Out New York, The Establishment, Role Reboot*, and the *Pleiades Book Review*. Other recent projects include co-authoring the exhibition catalog "Two American Poets: Wallace Stevens and William Carlos Williams" (Grolier Club, 2019) and composing the libretto for "Dreamless," a one-act opera that premiered at the Capital Fringe Festival in 2018.

Katie has taught creative writing, composition, research writing, and rhetoric at Emerson College, Roosevelt University, and the University of Wisconsin-Eau Claire. She has also led poetry workshops at the Cambridge Center for Adult Education, the Newberry Library, the Loft Literary Center, and ArtStart's School of the Arts Legacy Program. Currently, she teaches a monthly poetry class hosted by Gris Literatura.

When she's not writing or teaching, Katie can often be found singing with her band, The Flaming Doublewides, or serving on the Board of the Saint Paul Almanac. She lives in Minneapolis with her husband, Jake, and their cat, George Muffins. To learn more, please visit katievagnino.com.

CPSIA information can be obtained
at www.ICGtesting.com
Printed in the USA
BVHW030238030921
615864BV00003B/189